THE CROWN AND THE QUEEN

The Crown and The Queen

Queen Elizabeth II's Story, From a Century Back

Author: Natasha Tristan

Dedication

Dedicated to Almighty.

DISCLAIMER

The information provided in this book is best prepared from our knowledge and methods of findings. We have made every effort to ensure the accuracy and reliability of the details given in this. Anyhow, the information is included "as is" without any warranty of any kind. We do not assume any responsibility or obligation for the accuracy, content, completeness, legitimacy, and reliability of the information consisted in this book.

Acknowledgments

Greatly thankful to everyone for their immense support for the release of this book.

CONTENTS

CONTENTS

Queen Elizabeth II: Deserving the title of Iron Lady from the British Monarchy

The stories begin centuries ago. By an approximation, it can be said to be from 925-939 AD. That period was the beginning of the British monarchy or the British Royal family, which is on the steps of fame today. The British monarchy originated from small kingdoms in Anglo-Saxon England and early medieval Scotland. By the 10th century, it had been unified into the kingdoms of England and Scotland. Athelstan (895-939 AD) of House of Wessex, the grandson of Alfred the Great and the 30th great-granduncle of Queen Elizabeth II, was the first king of the entire England. The Anglo-Saxon-king defeated the last Viking invaders and ruled from 925-939 AD. The rule was to start with Athelstan and pass through many and reach in the hands of George VI. After his death at the age of 56, his daughter Queen Elizabeth II was crowned as the Ruler of England at Westminster Abbey on June 27, 1953, when she was 27 years old. It was there that the beginning of an unprecedented new era and the emergence of a new star.

At the age of 95, Queen Elizabeth II clings to the reign of England, which came to her hands at the age of 27, and she preserves what her forefathers entrusted to her, more beautiful than before, without giving it a bad name. Despite the old age that dominated her, she did not lose her old radiance, and with the beauty that old age instilled in her, she remained in power for almost 70 years from the time she was crowned.

She alone has many features that set Queen Elizabeth II apart from successive rulers.

Chapter 1- Military uniform within the monarchy

Looking back over the years, and just pausing in the United Kingdom of 1949, one can see the lesser participation of women in the armed forces. As World War II raged and its aggression was dragging on and slowly crawled to its end, she raised her head from the crowd to the military and gave her consent, despite opposition, when more force was needed. She bravely stepped forward and began to work from among those who were stunned by such an unexpected move. The reason for such a miracle among those people was that women from the royal family rarely entered the defense. The fame of being the first royal lady to serve in the army full time became her own throughout that action.

The legacy of military service in the British monarchy has long been ingrained. But Queen Elizabeth II was the first to rise from the head of state to such a responsibility, as the involvement of women from the royal family in World War II was deplorable. As the ravages of war intensified in every nook and corner of Europe, everyone, regardless of age, gender, creed, came forward to defend their homeland. When such a compulsion became necessary, men, women, farmers, businessmen, all began to be involved in warfare. It was then that Princess Elizabeth joined those who were ready to fight for the country, without just looking at everything and turning to one side in the power of her royal position. Thus she worked differently from the rest of the royal family. Like her father, who served in World War 1, she joined on her 18th birthday despite her heir to the throne and her father's reluctance. Over that action, words were raised openly and secretly from within the palace itself of mocking and criticizing her deed from many angles. She did not pay much attention to it. Princess Elizabeth enrolled in the Women's Auxiliary Territorial Service (ATS), similar to the American Women's Army Corps, Where women actively participate in valuable supportive roles. The overall responsibilities of ATS were radio operators, anti-aircraft gunners, and spotlight operators. From all this, the duties assigned to her were like that of mechanics and drivers. It was not a position that could be enjoyed in a very festive and luxurious way. As she was ready to be a part of the struggle, she became one of them and helped them as much as she could with her efforts, thus she had got a rough picture of their plight, security of the nation, and other similar problems. These experiences were like a training ground for her, and perhaps all of this would have helped her when she began to rule after being crowned head of the country in the future. The work she undertook in that war was difficult. Therefore, she did not accept the title of mechanic herself without even changing a tire symbolically. Her sincerity was evident through it. She took her work seriously and performed it spectacularly. She was proud to be involved in such commitments and she contributed the best of the service she could be. Gradually she learned to drive all the vehicles she worked for, including ambulances and the Tilly light truck. In that behavior, one can see her quality of quest to get a deeper understanding of everything that she interacts with closely.

She was only 19 years old when she joined the women's wing of the British Army at the height of World War II. Her decision to embark on such a large mission at such a young age was met with comments from several directions that it was a foolish act and a mistake. She stood firm in her stand. The fame of a Princess or Queen to begin her relationship with the Armed Forces was started from her in the British monarchy. The Queen has a very close and long connection with the Armed Forces of the United Kingdom and the Commonwealth. The closeness of

The Queen with the Armed Forces was maintained through her regular visits to service establishments and ships. She holds numerous military appointments and honorary ranks. The Queen's birthday is celebrated every year with a grand military parade of Trooping of the Color, just like the tradition of the monarch's birthday. For years, The Queen wore a military uniform and did Trooping on horseback. Refreshing her memory of her days working in the military, she spends a good deal of time with servicemen and women of all ranks, and their families, often at home or on overseas trips. In addition to presenting various military honors on investments, The Queen also introduced Elizabeth Cross. After all, she did not reject those who were martyred in the poison of war spit. The Queen's first medal was established in 2009 to give special recognition and honor to the families of those who have died in military action or due toin the aftereffect of terrorism from 1948. The Queen's act of supporting the families and loved ones of those heroes who sacrificed their lives for the welfare of the country was eye-opening.

The Queen arranged the medal as the form of the recognition, the Elizabeth Cross, as she got inspired by the precursors of the First and Second World Wars. Apart from these honors, The Queen leads the country to pay homage with respect to those war heroes on Remembrance Sunday every year.

On VE (Victory of Europe) Day, Princess Elizabeth went out with her sister in the crowd with the desire to be a part of the celebration. Tears of joy flowed from her as she realized the triumph of suffering. No one recognized the Princesses, who disguised themselves and shared time with them at the celebration at the end of the war. She was also involved later in the struggle for the country and was ordained to the role of Queen of England within a decade.

Why?

What you have read so far were the events of when Princess Elizabeth entered in her teens to the military as the war ignited heavily. Why did she join the Armed Forces at the time she had to sleep soundly on the silk mattress of the palace, weaving sweet dreams? Does that not leave you with doubt? Let's take a look at its background.

World War II, which lasted from 1939 to 1945, kept everyone's day and night in the caves of fear. It had no distinction of Royal family or subjects. As mentioned earlier, Princess Elizabeth received the ruler's crown at the age of 27, because she came to such a role as the heir to her father and King, George VI, following his untimely death. It only became 3 years into his reign King George VI on 3rd September 1939, it was the time that the Second World War trumpeted its horn, and The Princess was only 19 years old at that time when she joined the military. King George VI unexpectedly succeeded to the throne in 1936 following the abdication of his brother King Edward VIII. Thus, on September 3, 1939, at 6 pm, in his radio broadcast, King George VI spoke to the people of Britain and the Empire in detail about the war that was about to break out in front of them, and about the need to be vigilant in it. As the crucial situations prepared to conquer them, the King had to handle the ranks such as Admiral of the Fleet, Field Marshal, and Marshal of the Royal Air Force (RAF) also. As a follow-up, the King and Queen Elizabeth inspected the troops, visited workplaces, and assessed the then conditions. At that time, the King was in his uniform to observe everything. During the Blitz German bombing campaign against the United Kingdom in 1940 and 1941, the King and

Queen visited the bombarded areas devastated by the enemy air raids. In that attack, many helpless people, who had lost their homes, health, and loved ones, caught their eye. During those visits, the Queen was deeply hurt when she saw such people, and she became very interested in the thought of what could be done for them. The King traveled to visit troops in France and North Africa also. By 13 September 1940, Buckingham Palace had also been bombed. The strongest blows against the palace were nine times. The enemy invaded the country from all sides and scattered the dust of losses. The King and Queen took a keen interest in the works that people were engaged in and it energized them on the journey ahead. In each of their actions, they tried their best to show the rulers that the subjects are the source of the nation's power. When they saw the smile of satisfaction felt by the King and Queen on their actions, the morale of the people rose and the enthusiasm of the factory workers to do work also increased. When the Ministry of Supply examined the aftermath of the royal visits, they found that the rate of production during those visits had dropped but the figures for weekly production had risen unchanged.

Princesses Elizabeth and Margaret lived mostly in Windsor Castle during wartime. Amid those problems, their peers spent time with their parents, but when their friends experienced such relief, the Princesses had to stay away from their parents for many days. Despite haunting all those little minds, then Princess Elizabeth, who was only 14-year-old and mature enough to face the situation, broadcasted a message through the radio program, Children's Hour, in October 1940, to provide courage on her part for the helpless people. It's an instance of that the helping mentality is rooted in her at a young age.

Thus, Princess Elizabeth (Queen Elizabeth II) then fixed her legs to the arena of the military at the age of 19, joined the ATS, and served as a driver and mechanic in the rank of Second Subaltern. As she continued to be active in it, one morning five months later, she was given the new responsibility of Junior Commander, who was equivalent to the Captain. It was the recognition that came to her for acting sincerely without the arrogance of power. Her younger sister, Princess Margaret, was a Girl Guide, and later she joined as one of the members of Sea Rangers. As the days passed by, as the war began to touch the shores of its end, on May 8, 1945, at 6 pm on VE Day, the King again addressed the nation and arranged another broadcast. In the afternoon and evening, the King and the Royal Family gathered eight times on the balcony of Buckingham Palace to pay their respects of gratitude and to acknowledge the crowd for their services. King George VI had set the George Medal and George Cross to honor those who fought hard along with them. When the Royal Family joined together at the balcony to honor the crowd, Princess Elizabeth wore her military uniform with the male members of the family. When the atmosphere of serenity illuminated the white color of peace, the Princesses were able to secretly take part in all with them on the night of the mob's celebration.

Following the death of King George VI on February 6, 1952, Queen Elizabeth II came to power. She was off for two months on her 26th birthday and was on a royal trip in Kenya with her husband Prince Philip, at the time of her father's demise. Unfortunately, being unreachable, she was unlucky enough as a daughter to be part of the ceremony with her physical presence. A letter was sent from Buckingham Palace to the royal couple informing her of her dad's death but had not reached them. It was only when Elizabeth's private secretary finally got the information through a local journalist that they both came to know about the incident. By then it was too late. Prince Philip's inquiry into its authenticity was confirmed by hearing the BBC World Service on the radio. Through Ingrid Seward's biography, Prince Philip Revealed, it was uncovered the details to the outer world that Prince Philip told the Queen of her father's death while they were in Kenya.

Chapter 2 - Naughty or Polite?

Queen Elizabeth II has the face of a long-reigning ruler, who serves in the kingdom even in her 95th age approaching the 70 years of her coronation. Queen Elizabeth II was born as the eldest daughter of King George VI and Queen Elizabeth I, on April 21, 1926, in Mayfair, London, United Kingdom. She was lucky enough to set a record of the longest-reigning monarch in British history. Although she has witnessed changes in her reign as political changes have swept the world and the United Kingdom over time, she has always been able to leave a lasting impression on everyone's minds. When Elizabeth Alexandria Mary was born, her grandfather, King George V, was King of the United Kingdom (He was the Duke of York, Prince Albert, before his coronation). She was born a princess, as her father held the position of Duke of York at the time. Growing up, Elizabeth was nicknamed "Lilibet" by everyone. Despite being the princess of the United Kingdom, Elizabeth lived a simple life. Then the days went by and when it was time for her education, it was not allowed for the kids in the Royal Family to go to school like everyone else and study with others. But she was not denied the opportunity to study. She was educated at home by private tutors. She used to enjoy horse riding at her family's country home in Windsor Great Park. Her younger sister, Princess Margaret, was born on 21st August 1930, giving her an opportunity allowing her to become an elder sister. So the family became close again. Elizabeth was not a child of childhood mischief or childish behavior. Everyone who came in contact with her commented that she was decent, mature, and had a good foundation at such a young age. Elizabeth and her sister spent most of their childhood in a large house in London at 145 Piccadilly and at White Lodge in Richmond Park. It was only after her father, King George VI, ascended the throne that her life began to take a different turn. Due to her father's promotion, the family had to move their privacy to Buckingham

Palace, the royal residence in London. As the eldest of two children, Elizabeth was convinced that one day she will have to receive the crown. Her parents decided to make her aware of the special responsibilities and duties that would befall on her in the hope that she would become a future Queen. However, when they flew to Australia to open the new Commonwealth Parliament, she spent her early days with her nanny, Clara Knight, and grandparents King George V, and Queen Mary. Made saddened by the people who rumored that it might negatively affect her behavior, it increased her attachment with her grandparents.

Princess Elizabeth was enjoying the colorful period of her life with the elderly couple. The little girl was able to make their leisure time attractive to them. Instead, she was able to copy good qualities and values from them. When her parents returned from Australia in June 1927, they realized the result of it and smiled with satisfaction. When seeing their daughter again days after by her parents, they could observe the traits of love and confidence in her character. What they could see in her physical appearance was that she had become a beauty with chubby cheeks. She climbed up onto the table before being bombarded with fireworks her mother had distributed to welcome guests to that year's Christmas party in Sandringham! Even the king was not free from Elizabeth's game at that moment, and it took some time for the fear to go away from that stalemate. For a while, the atmosphere was entirely calm and shivering. Attending an audience with George V, the Archbishop of Canterbury once panicked when he saw King pretending to be a four-legged horse and Elizabeth playing the groom.

A few days later, things went on unchanged, and in 1930, her little sister Margaret was born, welcoming a new guest into their home. Five years have passed with that baby's play and laughter, and as the days and nights of 1936 fell apart, the changes began to occur around young Princess Elizabeth. On 20 January 1936, King George V went on a journey to a world of eternity where a return was impossible. Elizabeth still continued her education at home, shattering York's expectations that she would attend a public school to develop intellectually and socially. After George V's death, the crown was inherited by his eldest son, Edward VIII. He was the brother of Princess Elizabeth's father George VI. When Edward VIII came to power, he was opposed to leaving the princess to educate the common people. So Elizabeth continued her studies at home. He made that decision to protect their privacy. He calculated that such a move would reduce the penetration of press media into the Royal Family. Such a stance may seem like a cruel decision to most people, doesn't it? Most of the comforts that children outside the palace can enjoy were not able to experience for the kids in the Royal Family. There was an incident that prompted Edward VIII to be behind his strict decision on Princess' education. He caught the attention that the national gossip has a significant role in spreading his relationship with the socialite Wallis Simpson before her marital status came to light. That's why he feared the media and became concerned about the matter of education. During the last days of 1937, the pages turned to irrecoverable occurrences in Elizabeth's life. With the abdication of Edward VIII, her father King George VI came to power. Naturally, she was the Heiress to Throne after him as the eldest child in the family. Knowing that she would be the head of the Monarchy in the future, she began to understand the duties she had to deal with since she was very young. She learned the lessons of constitutional history from Eton. As European History became one of her favorite topics, she began to grasp knowledge about it at a deeper level. Her studies narrowed down due to the events unfolding under Hitler's leadership in 1939. In the heat of the war, Elizabeth and Margaret had to be relocated to Canada. But as soon as such a discussion started, their mother rejected the idea. They said that the children would not leave her, that she could not stay away from the King, and that the King would never leave them. So, the curtain fell on that plan. So what finally happened after the talks was that the princesses first spent days at Balmoral and then followed by Sandringham and lastly pushed out their days in Windsor. When the princesses returned to their place, Elizabeth decided to enter into her responsibilities. Before that, she was part of a series of national visits with the King and Queen to strengthen her morale. So, for the first time, when she was about to face public appearances alone, in 1943, at the age of 16, she also met Grenadier Guards. Shortly before her 18th birthday, she also got the opportunity to become one of the five Counsellors of State who visited the Italian battlefields in July 1944. This was followed by her grand entry into the Armed Forces and all the related events. Thus the war continued vigorously, Hitler died and the cool atmosphere was filled with the scent of peace at the end of the war. After all, she went to South Africa in 1947 for her first official visit. At the end of the year, she took the pledge of dedication to the people of the Commonwealth.

At a young age, she practiced fighting techniques for survival. She began her survival skills training as the Girl Guide, the U.K. version of Girl Scouts. Her mother was already its supporter and along with mother, her sister Margaret also followed it, so at age 11, Princess Elizabeth joined them. Though it had arranged a facility called 1st Buckingham Palace Company but as she could not attend any of the schools, Elizabeth joined Girl Guides to meet her peers. Princess Elizabeth can even see in a 1943 picture practicing her bandaging skill on her sister. She found time to join Sea Rangers, a team that teaches sailing and other water-based activities.

Chapter 3 - New Beginning in Princess Elizabeth's life

The period of 1934. It was a time when the heroine of the palace was only eight years old. Two distant cousins, aged eight and thirteen, met for the first time at the wedding of Princess Marina of Greece and Denmark to Prince George and Duke of Kent. Little did they know when they stood together in their playful moments that day that in the future they would be sharing a lifetime together. Coincidentally, in the tender age, the future couple Queen Elizabeth II and Prince Philip marked their first encounter without realizing it. They both were the great-great-grandchildren of Queen Victoria. It was not until 1939 that they met again. At the second meeting, the old kids, Princess Elizabeth was 13 and Prince Philip of Greece (at the time) was 18. The second meeting happened when Elizabeth visited the Royal Navy College at Dartmouth with her family, where Prince was training as a cadet. Between those sounds, a silent love blossomed there. Marion Crawford, the Queen's nanny at the time, realized this and wrote in their book, about the closeness of Prince and Queen. She described it in an interesting way as that the Queen never took her eyes from the Prince. In the years that followed, their contact was through correspondence. Then her eyes did not pass on to anyone else for a romantic affair. They began to know each other better through the words in the letters. Through the letters, they madly loved each other. Their bond became so strong as to be inseparable. Although the Prince did not have the technical privilege of marrying someone in the position of Queen at the time, King George VI liked him as his son-in-law. He asked them to wait a year for the Queen to turn 21 before deciding on an engagement. It was in 1946 that the Prince received the blessings of the king to own his love. Then he felt a desire to make a proposal to his love who had already decided by all as his own. Philip proposed to her during a month-long vacation at Balmoral with her family.

One year later, in 1947, as they had already decided, the process of officially announcing their relationship began. The times they got in between added to the brilliance of their sweet romantic moments. Thus ending their beautiful years of waiting, Queen Elizabeth and Prince Philip finally announced their engagement on July 9, 1947. When they thought about how to make variety in the engagement ring, London jeweler Philip Antrobus came up with a solution to those confusions. He presented a different idea that it could be created using the diamonds in her mother's tiara, and he made it to everyone's liking.

At first the Queen's family had only little interest in their union. One reason is that his royal house, which was exiled from Greece, was experiencing poverty then. The other was that the closeness his siblings had with the Nazis. His sisters were married to them. So the brightness of the dreams they saw together was increasing. Everything has reached the point where they can get married soon without delaying their long wait again. The wedding of Princess Elizabeth with Prince Philip was the first major event to take place there after the attack by World War II. Westminster Abbey witnessed that great ceremony. The King insisted them to conduct the marriage in a small and peaceful manner without showing too much luxury. The wedding of the Queen and the Prince was attended by only 2000 guests. After that, a luncheon was arranged at Buckingham Palace. Through this ceremony, they showed that a marriage in the Royal Family could be so simple. It was on 20 November 1947 that the Queen and Prince happily joined their relationship with a function called marriage. A 9-foot-tall wedding cake was cut for the reception. After the wedding celebrations, the couple went on a honeymoon trip to Broadlands, the Prince's family estate in Hampshire, to collect and remember their good moments. When the King and queen decided to announce the betrothal of their Princess, Philip became a British citizen and adopted the name "Mountbatten." Just before their wedding, he was given the role of Duke of Edinburgh. The problem that bothered everyone when setting their wedding date was money. The nation was slowly recovering from the wounds of war. Food was available in moderation in the country. Imports of petrol, tobacco, and paper were restricted. In short, it was not possible to have an immediate marriage in a way that would highlight the status of the Royal Family. It was considered a cost-cutting wedding, so the government gifted Princess Elizabeth an extra 200 clothing coupons for her dress. She tried to wear a beautiful attire for a wedding that was supposed to be so simple and for the money available considering the limited financial status. She chose an ivory silk gown sewn with thousands of seed pearls. Due to the rationing of World War II, Queen Elizabeth II saved up the clothing coupons to pick up her wedding dress. Many people who were attracted to the young Royal bride sent their coupons by mail, but they had to return them as it was illegal. When the future Queen finally received her dress, the bridal attire was 13 feet in length and decorated with 10,000 seed pearls and adorned it very beautifully. In that ivory gown made by 350 women in seven weeks, in its elegant and dazzling features even in its simplicity, Elizabeth looked so gorgeous. It was Philip that obeyed closely to the austerity mandate. Some reports said that the Duke of Edinburgh, who was always indifferent to clothes and fond of economization, took off his naval uniform and wore adorned socks to Westminster Abbey. But the snapping of the diamond tiara of Princess Elizabeth caused a little pain in the midst of joyous events. Her mother, The Queen, calmed everyone down by calling a court jeweler to repair it. The Queen promised everyone that it would be fixed. Her belief went right. The circumstances in which the two grew up were different. Philip, who was handsome and an athlete, led a worldly life. When his Royal Family was forced to flee his native Greece, they shifted alternately like migratory birds and having lived in Paris, the United Kingdom, and Germany. For one thing, it can be found similarity in their upbringing, with both of them, spent most of their childhood apart from their parents. He served in the furnace of the Second World War in the Mediterranean and the Pacific. Looking at Elizabeth's educational affairs, she never left the U.K., studies were at home itself. She was very fluent in French. Elizabeth's letter of 1947 indicates that after the war she and Philip really had many moments to share together. When he stayed at a school of naval officers, he tried to spend weekends to celebrate and a long break with the Queen and her family. There were rumors that their different backgrounds were causing concern to others in the royal family.

According to Clive Irving, the author of 'The Last Queen: How Queen Elizabeth II Saved the Monarchy', that before their marriage, there were doubts as to whether Philip was the half who suits Princess. It was the annoying memories of the case of Edward VIII and Wallis Simpson that fueled such thinking. At the time, Edward VIII was leaving the monarchy instead of giving her up. Shortly after their marriage, she wrote to her family that they still behaved as if they had been together for years and that Philip was a good personality of having a thoughtful mind and being kind. She added that he was like an Angel. Philip withdrew his royal title of Duke of Edinburgh and enjoyed private life with his young wife. As she took her life to a fresh lesson, Elizabeth sent a letter of happiness about her new life as a relief for the tensions her family had experienced, along with her, Philip also wrote words for his new mother-in-law. When it comes to the content of his letter, his desire is two weld the two together into a new combined existence, not only to deal with the impacts on all of them, but also to ensure that the good will have a good existence. Elizabeth's father, King George VI, had expressed a similar way. In a letter to his daughter after her marriage, he praised his love for her and also expressed how much he misses her. He reminded her that he could see that she was very happy with Philip, and that it was true, but she should not forget her parents.

What is interesting about this is that if the letters acted as messengers for their romance before marriage, then after marriage the letter had to act as a mediator of communication with their family. For a time, their lives were filled with a series of letters.

Their wedding was watched by people all over the world through BBC broadcast and it was celebrated as an international event. The good news reached them, leading them on new missions in their lives that were happily moving forward like the calm flow of a river. Elizabeth gave birth to their first child, Prince Charles, on November 14, 1948, taking the couple's days to a new level. The baby was born in Buckingham Palace. By August 15, 1950, Princess Anne had joined them as their second child in Clarence House. Prince Andrew in 1960 and Prince Edward were again added like the hatching of two little birds to their family tree, known as the Windsor Family.

When evaluating a mother named Elizabeth, it cannot be said completely that she is uncaring. The hectic schedule of dealing with the roles of a ruler, spouse, and mother at the same time may have been such as to keep her away from her children. It was while trying to secure the first steps to a quiet married life that the responsibilities as a monarch unexpectedly struck over her head. So when she started to carry the burden of it, at first there may have been very small adjustments in her personal life to bring everything into a balance. So she often had less time to spend with her children, especially with the elder kids, Charles and Anne. As part of her duties as a Queen, she had to think about the education of her children when she had to tour around the country and in most parts of the commonwealth. She recalled the circumstances of her childhood education in the fact that she was a member of a royal family and so had to study under private tutors inside the Palace. Therefore, she did not want to create such a condition for her children. As the children grew up,

Prince Philip and Queen Elizabeth II felt that it was better to teach their children at school with other children rather than at home. On such a decision, the children of the royal family spent most of the year away from home to study at boarding school. This was a setback for Prince Charles as he did not have a positive experience in boarding school. When the royal family was together, they enjoyed their family holidays at Balmoral and Sandringham. Their family photographs and films show that Prince Philip and Queen spent well with their children using the time whenever they get. Princess Anne spoke to the BBC in 2002 about it. She said that as children, she and siblings would not have asked for so much in the sense that they understood the limitations of time and the responsibilities imposed on Elizabeth and the travels she had to do as the monarch. She added that neither of them felt a second thought that she was not caring for them like any other mother. All this suggests that there was a strong family bond between the Windsors.

Chapter 4 - The Arrival of a new role

Queen Elizabeth II, who was living comfortably with children and husband, was unexpectedly invited to the role of managing responsibilities that would push her to royal duties. She used to expect it to approach anytime but she did not expect to have to deal with it suddenly during that family life. In 1951, King George VI's health began to decline, and he was unable to concentrate on his administration. Then as Elizabeth was the next heir to the throne, therefore she had to take on the duties that her father had to perform in his distress. Thus every task of the administration slowly began to reach under her. As part of that, in Trooping the Color, whom the king was supposed to attend, she represented him in it because he was unable to participate. She later became a regular member of state-related occasions. When getting a short break, Princess Elizabeth and her husband Prince Philip went on a successful tour of

Canada, Washington, and D.C. The couple began preparations for their next journey after Christmas in England. In January 1952, she and Duke set out on a tour of Australia and New Zealand. But on the way, their joy was dashed, and when they arrived in Sagana, Kenya, the news that King George VI had died on February 6, 1952, shook their ears. She was sad that she could not see her father for the last time. Elizabeth returned to England. Thus she became the head of the administration.

The first three months of her reign were spent mourning the death of her father, then came the days of comparatively calm and solitude. But during the summer, after she had shifted from Clarence House to Buckingham Palace, she started to take over her regular duties and under her presidency, opening the first State of Parliament on November 4, 1952. It was her first major state event before coronation. People thronged to see their new monarch on the traditional royal procession at the Palace of Westminster. With the exception of 1959 and 1963, all other Parliaments were opened by the Queen during her reign. The Queen was not available on both times, because at the time she was carrying Prince Andrew and Prince Andrew. There were only minor changes to the ceremonies throughout her reign.

Edward VIII was supposed to inherit the position as heir apparent at the time, but he was unable to take up the role again at that time because he had already left the role and was in trouble with the problems related to Wallis Simpson. That's how those responsibilities turned around and came to her.

Thus, finally, her official coronation to the title of the monarch of the United Kingdom took place in Westminster Abbey on June 2, 1953, festively.

Beginning in November 1953, the Queen and the Duke of Edinburgh toured the Commonwealth for six months all around the world, including in it, the first visit of a ruling British monarch To Australia and New

Zealand. Later she had to make her travels to be done mostly from the power of a ruler. After her state visits to several European nations, she and Duke visited Canada and the United States together in 1957. They enjoyed the rare few moments they got away from the hustle and bustle of the administration as their own. She then went on to make various tours differently from other rulers and achieved a number of records in her name. One of them was that in 1961, she made the first royal British tour of the Indian subcontinent in 50 years. And the next two tours she did were great to add to her credits, when looking at how it was, she was the first British monarch to visit South America and the Persian Gulf countries while reigning. At first, it was a continuous flow of letters after her marriage but when she came to power it was replaced by tours.

During her "Silver Jubilee" of 1977, she chaired a London banquet attended by 36 Commonwealth leaders. In her existing duties, she then held the position also for the first time.

The voyages did not end there, then she traveled throughout Britain and Northern Ireland. She has also been involved in regular tours to places like the Pacific, Canada, the Caribbean, and many other foreign countries.

With the accession of Queen Elizabeth II, naturally, as their eldest son, Prince Charles became the next heir to the throne. On July 26, 1958, he was named Prince of Wales. In 1987, the Queen's daughter, Princess Anne, was created as Princess Royal. Prince Andrew was created Duke of York in 1986 and Prince Edward was created Earl of Wessex and Viscount Severn in 1999. All of these kids have the surname "Windsor." But in 1960, Queen Elizabeth II decided to create the hyphenated name Mountbatten-Windsor for other successors of the style, such as Prince, Princess, and Royal Highness.

From the very beginning of the reign, as a ruler Elizabeth understood the importance of public relations. It was based on that thought that she decided to broadcast the coronation on television. However, Winston Churchill's team considered that this was undermining the value of coronation ceremonies.

Queen Elizabeth II, who crowned the 40th leader of the British Empire, performed well in the administration in which the nation ever experienced and also won a popular place among all. In 2003, she celebrated the 50th anniversary of her reign, which was celebrated only by the fifth King of England. When Elizabeth II was promoted to Queen's position after the war, several major kingdoms dominated England. Flags of peace were hoisted in many places so that in the 1950s and 1960s, many countries gained independence and breathed a sigh of relief. Finally, the British Empire evolved into the Commonwealth. Queen Elizabeth II, representing Britain, successfully made her first trip to Germany in 1965. When The Queen technically entered the position of Head of State of the British Government, she rarely interfered in politics. Queen, who showed no deep interest or had less knowledge of the area, was careful in politics during her reign and was involved in little unavoidable circumstances.

At the beginning of her tenure, she appointed a Prime Minister to form the government from the Conservative party. She was persuaded to this decision by the thought that she could not handle a section with which she was unfamiliar and could not bear the burden of it also. So she first chose Harold

Macmillan in 1957 and Alec Douglas-Home in 1963. As time went on, political parties began to adopt their own methods to select the Prime Minister. Although she did not express her involvement directly in politics, she did meet with the Prime Ministers every week to assess matters. Such meetings increased the space for them to discuss things carefully and made things easier. At such times, they would update the Queen of government and state affairs. In the early stages, when she was a young Queen and everything was unfamiliar to her, she was offered advice by Prime Ministers like Winston Churchill.

Chapter 5 - Her reign

Let's take a look at the important events that took place in her reign. It can be said that this is a reign where many important events broke out of the nest. An important one among them is already mentioned above, which is the selection of Prime Ministers.

The attack towards Egypt by the United Kingdom and France in an attempt to regain control over the Suez Canal in 1956 November was during the reign of Queen Elizabeth II. Britain, France, and Israel respond to the nationalization of the Suez Canal Company by a joint military operation by Egyptian President Nasser. What's its result? The last victory was for Egypt. The British, French and Israeli governments withdrew their troops in late 1956 and early 1957. It was later considered a political disaster and they had no choice but to concede defeat. It was a crisis that lasted from 29 October 1956 to 7 November 1956. It affected Britain. That led to a major political collapse there. On the one hand, the economic crisis was slowly rising. When evaluating its impact at an international level, it further complicated the politics of the Middle East. Britain's diplomatic relations with the Commonwealth nations and the 'special relationship' that existed between the United States-United Kingdom were threatened.

The next problem arose between the siblings. The affair of Queen Elizabeth II's sister, Margaret with a divorcee and Group Captain Peter Townsend was the news that created an effect like a major earthquake the day after the Queen's coronation. At the time, the Queen was the head of the Church of England which restricted remarriage with divorcees, so the relationship was highly discredited. There was a sense of tension between the two. Circumstances led them to a situation of a Queen and a citizen rather than as siblings. Margaret was still under the age of 25 and needed Elizabeth's permission to marry. For Elizabeth, their sisterhood was annulled by the Crown. The power made her confused as a barrier so that she could not show the sincerity of that relationship. But Margaret always gave priority to her sister. Margaret thought Elizabeth was her sister and that she had done anything for her and that she would always support Elizabeth. She was aware of the problems of getting married despite the opposition of the family. If Margaret and Townsend were trying to get married in any way without everyone's permission, the only way forward for them was a civil marriage. She realized that if that had happened then she would lose her income, her status as a member of the royal family, and her place in the line of succession. Margaret finally decided to honor her sister and Crown in her relationship with Townsend. Luckily for them, there was no rift in the sisterhood over her relationship with Townsend. Margaret thought intelligently and made a fair decision, everything was solved without any cracks. So it was buried between them as a closed, forgotten chapter. Finally, on May 6, 1960, Princess Margaret's wedding was solemnized in Westminster Abbey, London, with Antony Amstrong-Jones, a notable society photographer.

The rulers of Riyadh have been making occasional visits to the U.K. over years. One such was King Faisal of Saudi Arabia, who met Queen Elizabeth and Duke of Edinburgh in May 1967 at Buckingham Palace.

As a leader, she tried to do something in her reign, as well as she could in sports. An example of this was the opening of the Summer Olympics by Queen in 1976 in Montreal, Canada. During that time, she spent ten days in Quebec and Ontario. There was also the Queen's presence at the Olympic competitions. Princess Anne was a competitor in equestrian events. Prince Philip was behind until August 1, when the games ended. Thus the eventful history of the regime was celebrated in 1977 with the joy of the Silver Jubilee. Elizabeth could not have imagined that she would go so far as to unexpectedly receive the Queen's crown in sudden, fulfillment of which was evident in her. It was a celebration of the joy of a nation as a whole.

The 25th anniversary of Elizabeth II's royal entry into the throne as the head of the United Kingdom and other Commonwealth realms in 1977 was made grand with large-scale parties and parades across the U.K. and the Commonwealth. In June, the curtain fell on the celebration of "Jubilee Days" by holding programs in connection with the Queen's official birthday. To celebrate the silver jubilee of their beloved Queen's reign, everyone gathered all over the country during the festive season, day and night.

By 1979, the Queen's monarchy had witnessed the next historic moment. Margaret Thatcher became the first woman Prime Minister of the United Kingdom.

One of the most remarkable and popular events in history occurred in 1981. Prince Charles joined hands with Lady Diana as his better half that year. The relationship between Queen Elizabeth II and Lady Diana is worth mentioning. The bond between them was stronger than a mother-in-law and daughter-in-law. As Diana started living near the palace since her childhood, they have known each other for a long time. Later, when Prince Charles and Diana got into a relationship and they got married, that closeness between Elizabeth and Diana was still deep. The Queen's role in giving her mental support was not small, even when the couple parted ways over Camella's issue. Diana's death also deeply wounded her. The saddened face of Queen Elizabeth II on the death of Princess Diana was the headlines of the news those days.

The attainment in which a reigning Pope visited the United Kingdom for the first time became a reality during the reign of Queen Elizabeth II. The Queen happily welcomed the Pope on his visit to England in 1982. When the Pope arrived in the UK on May 28, he also visited nine cities. Along with it, he had delivered 16 major addresses. In addition to meeting with the Queen, he also met several other important personalities such as the Supreme Governor of the Church of England, Archbishop of Canterbury, Robert Runcie at Canterbury Cathedral, etc, and was a part of various events. During that six-day visit, which he set aside from his hectic schedules, he explored locations in England, Scotland, and Wales. The Pope's first destination on that tour was Westminster Cathedral, from where he entered the door of Buckingham Palace to see Queen Elizabeth II. On June 2 he returned to the Vatican.

Queen addressed a joint meeting of the United States Congress in 1991 following the victory of the Alliance in the Gulf War. The Times enthusiastically described the broadcast as 'unprecedented". The Queen herself took the initiative and spoke after consulting with Prime Minister John Major and government ministers before being broadcasted. The Queen said on an occasion that Allied's victory against the Iraqi forces will certainly be swift, and they can all pray together to achieve that at the lowest possible cost to human life and suffering. After speaking in-depth for a while, the Queen concluded that, following the victory, the real reward for their courage would be given to them that would bring about justice and lasting peace. The event took place on 24 February 1991, shortly before the end of the Gulf War.

Annus Horribilis

The year 1992 has left a lasting memory of shedding tears for the British Royal Family forever. This is especially painful for Queen Elizabeth II, who has been on the throne for years. Let's look at what was created for them that year to give all of them a roar of pain. It is sadly remembered as Annus Horribilis. Just like Prince Andrew and his wife Sarah, Duchess of York, the notable couple Prince Charles and his partner, Diana, Princess of Wales, were separated. Anne also got divorced and became a total mess. The royal residence of Windsor Castle was engulfed by fire. Elizabeth, on the other hand, was facing some other problems while the commotion of parting in the family was going on. In short, the Queen was the one who was haunted by everyone's problems. And as the country struggled with the recession, resentment over the royal family's lifestyle increased, and in 1992 Elizabeth, although privately excluded, agreed to pay taxes on her personal income. No matter how many years her reign had passed, it was 1992 that put her under a lot of pressure.

The Queen herself described the worst year as Annus Horribilis, a Latin word meaning 'horrible year'.

What hurt her most privately that year was the unexpected divorce in her children's lives. Prince Charles and his mate, Princess Diana, were equally dear to her. The Queen's joy knew no bounds when Diana, who had been on Elizabeth's list of favorites since childhood, was welcomed to a bond of daughter-in-law. But the dark shade suddenly fell on that happiness. How did the fence of the strong bond between Prince Charles and Princess Diana, who had been acquainted since childhood and turned into a love affair in adolescence, break down? An extramarital affair with Prince Charles and Camilla Parker Bowles broke up his relationship with Princess Diana. The ensuing depression in Diana plunged the Queen also into grief. Princess Diana remained involved in royal duties even after her divorce at the behest of the Queen.

It was Queen Elizabeth II who brought Diana and Charles, who were mentally estranged from Prince's relationship with Camilla, to a solution called divorce. She took such a step to avoid seeing that horrible pain of Diana whom she loved like a daughter. Many people said that Her Majesty had a cold attitude towards Diana during the period of divorce. But she was sympathetic to her. Even after separation, the Queen remained a pillar to provide Diana with mental support. More than sympathy, the Queen had affection for her.

The Queen's demeanor at the time made her understand that Queen Elizabeth II was a fair and just personality, albeit officially or personally. Because she did not shy away from her responsibilities even when private issues bothered her so much, she tried her best to manage both, despite the hardships. When all these problems somehow calmed down, on August 31, 1997, Lady Diana's death from a car crash pierced her ears. It froze her for a moment. She then forgot everything around her. To everyone's surprise, Queen Elizabeth II bowed at Princess Diana's funeral. The Queen said on the occasion that her death was a "shock and grief" and that her departure was a great loss to the country.

In 2002, the next chapter of losses re-opened in front of her. Her 101-year-old mother and 71-year-old sister Margaret said bye to her into a world of eternity where there is no return back. What prompted her to come out of the shock of those gaps was the reminder that it was the Golden Jubilee of her 50th year as she had set foot on the title of Queen of the United Kingdom. It made her realize that it was not right for her to show frustration in front of people who started the celebration in its joy. The Golden Jubilee event of Queen Elizabeth II's entry into the crown and Commonwealth realms was an international celebration. She considered it as the commemoration of the 50th anniversary of her being as a monarch and an opportunity to officially and personally thank them for their loyalty. Because of the death of her mother and sister, who died in February and March 2002 respectively, thought to not have to make a grand event, but London celebrated the Jubilee on a large scale in June. She traveled about 40,000 miles with Prince Philip, Duke of Edinburgh as part of the celebration as scheduled. The royal couple journeyed to the Caribbean, Australia, New Zealand, around the United Kingdom, and finally, put the curtain on her jubilee year in Canada.

The sixth session of the Scottish Parliament was officially opened by the Queen at Holyrood on October 9, 2004. Construction of the building began in June 1999, with the Members of the Scottish Parliament holding their first debate in the new building on 7 September 2004.

The wedding of Prince William, Queen Elizabeth II's grandson and second heir apparent to the British throne, with Catherine, Duchess of Cambridge, took place on 29 April 2011 in Westminster Abbey, London.

The year 2012 in British history marked the 60th anniversary of her standing on the throne of a monarch as the next shining milestone in the reign of Queen Elizabeth II. Before Elizabeth, Queen Victoria was the only ancestor who crossed the 60th year of the accession to the throne and thus celebrated the Diamond Jubilee. Thus, in 2015, at the age of 89, she won the recognition of the longest-reigning monarch in British history.

Queen Elizabeth II reached that position by surpassing the record of her great-great-grandmother Queen Victoria's longest stay on the throne. The record previously held by Queen Victoria was that she reigned for 63 years and 217 days. But wiping it all out, she entered the crown in 1952 after her marriage to Prince Philip, and continues to rule, attracting huge attention. She showed her presence to this title when she was just 25 years old.

While the Diamond Jubilee celebrations for her crown were going on as usual in 2015, the Queen inaugurated a new train in Scotland. She used the ceremony to offer her gratitude to all those who worked for her and to her well-wishers. With previous experience in defense, she served in 2019 as Commander-in-Chief of the British Armed Forces and the Canadian Armed Forces.

Photography is a favorite hobby of Queen Elizabeth II, but not much noticed by the outside world. She maintains a strict schedule even as she reaches the peak of her old age. She stands with grace in all great tensions and still expresses her love for dogs and horses even in the oldness with great interest. Since she is famous for her many achievements and good deeds and has spent most of her life in front of public space, many books have been published about her official and private life. Photography was more of a sentimental gift from her father than a hobby she inherited when she was just a young child. It is said that King George VI gave her a camera before World War II made its noises. So she likes to copy images of her friends and family with her click. She often captures animals, landscapes, and special events through the lens of her camera.

Like photography, pets were something she loved. Her favorite dogs were corgis. She has owned more than 30 of them since she reigned as Queen. In one fell swoop she gained 13 of them. She loves corgis very much, so she considers them as her family. From Charles I's spaniel to Victoria's favorite dog, Dash, they were all loyal companions for the British royal family. Overcoming all these, Queen Elizabeth II raised the corgis of 14 generations. She has cared for more than 30 corgis for the past 70 years. She loves corgis more than any other breed because of its energy and unrestrained spirit. The relationship between Elizabeth and corgis began in 1933 when they welcomed the first corgis, Dookie, into the royal family. Willow, the last surviving member of the royal corgis' family, died of cancer in April 2018, much to the disappointment of the Queen. After that, she got a few with furry. She got a new corgi for her birthday in 2021. She felt excited as if she had been brought back to life. The story of the Queen's fondness with pets thus goes on.

Benefits as the head of state

Queen Elizabeth II is also credited with being the most traveled head of the state. The same is true whether it is official or private. With more than 270 official visits, she has been able to visit over 115 countries. But what is surprising above all is that she does not have a passport of her own. How is this possible? All British passports were officially issued in the Queen's name, so technically she did not need one. Because she held such a privileged position, she was still entitled with many benefits. In Britain, the driver's license was also issued with Elizabeth's name. So she does not have to show her ID while carrying other heads of states in her Range Rover. She does not even need a driving license. She did not have to pay tax, but in some cases did not comply (that instance was mentioned earlier). Since 1982, she has voluntarily paid income and capital gains taxes. But always subject to Value Added Taxes.

Slipping away from death

It is not uncommon for ruling elites to be attacked by those who do not like their growth or who do not like their way of governing. But can you believe that there have been attempts to attack the popular Queen Elizabeth II? Not to wonder, it's true. Not once or twice, but three times did she just escape death.

Queen Elizabeth II's trip to Australia in 1970 was a much awaited event with Prince Philip. At that moment, an attack on the Queen erupted. It had been found by former Detective Superintendent Cliff McHardy. Monarch and her husband were scheduled to leave Sydney on April 29 for a trip to Orange in New South Wales. As they went near Lithgow, a log had set up on the train track in an attempt to derail the locomotive, and McHardy told Macquarie Radio that it was probably the killers. An hour before the queen's train arrived, another train track was inspected, but none of them were found to be abnormal, after that which the log is found, which strengthened the suspicion that it might be an assassination attempt. The train, which was traveling by the monarch, collided with the log, but was reported to be moving too slowly to repair the damage. But the perpetrators were not caught, and the truth came out only when McHardy remembered it at his retirement ceremony in 2009. His opinion is that the government hid it to avoid embarrassment.

An assassination attempt was made towards her during the Trooping the Color of 1981. It's an annual event organized in London. The shots sounded at her as she rode her horse from Mall to Buckingham Palace in a royal procession. When you hear all this, if you think an adult acted against the Queen, then you are mistaken. Elizabeth was repeatedly shot by a 17-year-old Marcus Sarjeant who was obsessed with the murders of John F. Kennedy and John Lennon. He fired six blanks from a starting pistol. This horrific event took place on June 13, 1981, which brought everyone to a standstill. Death passed her by untouched. It was something that shook the country. He was sentenced to five years in prison under the

Treason Act of 1848, and was released in October 1984.

Queen Elizabeth II met death face-to-face again in the same year, 1981. She was attacked a few months after the assassination attempt on her at the Mall. That happened when she visited New Zealand in 1981 to see the museum in the city of Dunedin. The culprit was a 17-year-old Christopher John Lewis. He was hiding in a nearby building and opened fire through the windows when the queen placed her legs out of her vehicle. But his attempt did not bear fruit. Witnesses to the incident later described the sound as a "loud crack" with a frightened face. Eight days later he was arrested. He was also partially housed in a mental health facility for three years.

The entry of an intruder

Her Majesty escaped the assassination attempts by a slight difference and was next caught in the hands of an intruder in the very next year 1982. Previously, she had received threats outside Buckingham Palace or elsewhere, but this time it was inside the Palace.

On June 9, 1982, a man named Michael Fagen climbed over a barbed wire fence in the Palace, then stepped up a drain pipe, and finally entered into the Queen's bedroom unnoticed. Some reports at the time said that he had been in a conversation with the Queen for a long time before being caught by security at the Palace. It was not clear whether Fagen's actions were part of an assassination attempt, a conspiracy or something else.

Eternal farewell of Queen's love

Prince Philip retired from his public life in August 2017. After that, he did not want to waste time and started seeing him in official engagements from time to time. At such times, the Queen would shorten the length of her duties and could divide it between Prince Charles and other senior members of the royal family.

Charles' youngest son, Prince Harry, Duke of Sussex, and his wife, Meghan, Duchess of Sussex, relinquished their royal duties in March 2020 that were assigned to them. Public interest in the royal family and the Queen grew during that period, and the Windsors became known around the world through The Crown, which aired in 2016 on the Netflix television series.

Prince Philip, who had been suffering with several health problems in recent years, surrendered to death in April 2021. The demise of the better-half, who had been her pillar for more than seven decades, plunged the Queen into the abyss of grief. She slowly survived from his death, as she learned to cope up with that emptiness by adding down the names of each of her loved ones, often in a book of losses. Queen Elizabeth II praised Prince Philip in 1997 at their 50th wedding anniversary celebration as that he was very simple and that he was very simple and also that he was her power and had stood by hers so for long.

As an individual

Queen Elizabeth II favors simplicity in court life. She takes a serious approach to government business, aside from traditional and ritualistic responsibilities. She can be considered as one of the richest women in the world in terms of her financial and property assets. It doesn't mean that she is the richest person in Britain.

Based on the estimates of American Magazines, Times and Forbes, she has an economic worth of $480 and $500 million respectively. But that's still below the richest people's magazine's list of 2,674 billionaires in 2021. Most of the Queen's personal wealth comes from estates.

Attractive unknown faces of Queen

A trait that sets Queen Elizabeth II apart from others is that of utilizing her own ways to help the poor. She did not depend on the monarchy's savings collection to fulfill her wish. It is known as 'Maundy

Money" in their style. The Queen has silver coins in her possession and would often give them to pensioners at the ceremony called Maundy Thursday. It was something that had to be done with respect.

The event followed the customs of the 13th century. The Royal Family imitated the Bible as they washed the feet of the penniless and gave them presents considered as a symbolic expression of Jesus Christ washing and honoring the feet of the poor. Once the scrolls of the 18th century were unrolled, it was found that washing the dirty feet of the poor was not suited for the royal, and instead of it, the money bequeathed by the monarch was distributed as allowances.

The next variety that makes a difference for others in empress is that she is celebrating two birthdays. The Queen was born on April 21, 1926, but no official celebrations were held until the second Saturday in June. It was a tradition introduced by King George II in 1748 and has remained unchanged over time. The reason behind this is that he was born in November but later decided to celebrate it on another day in the same year, saying that there would be no public celebrations that time as its weather wasn't good. Another little known thing is that the Queen had her personal fashion designer.

After a series of commissions for the royal family, the task was assigned to a designer Norman Hartnell. The hands behind the beautification of the Queen's wedding gown and coronation attire were his. It is said to have been portrayed as a protagonist in over 200 films and TV series. The Queen first sent an email on March 26, 1976. She was then at the Royal Signals and Radar Establishment, a telecommunications research centre in Malvern. That email opened the way for a new programming language. It was the first email sent from a royal.

Elizabeth owned a house when she was just six years old. A house named Y Bwthyn Bach, which means 'little cottage", was on the grounds of the Windsor

Royal Lodge and in which it was gifted to her by people in Wales. She has several residences across the country, including Windsor Castle and Buckingham Palace, but this is special that made her a homeowner at just six years old.

There were some assets that were inherited from her father and became privately owned properties for the Queen. They are Sandringham House in Norfolk and Balmoral Castle, Craigowan Lodge and Delnadamph Lodge. There are reports that she drinks a glass of champagne every night before going to bed. Then there is a private ATM facility at Buckingham Palace that the Queen can only use. It is facilitated by Coutts, one of the most popular banks in Great Britain. She is often said to have used her purse to secretly pass signals to her staff. Every Christmas, millions in Britain and 54 Commonwealth nations eagerly await the Christmas message of the monarch.

The Queen owned all the swans and dolphins in the waters of the U.K. The Queen would not eat any swans later, but would technically own them all. Someone has specially arranged to take care of it. Every year the Queen's Swan Marker conducts a multi-day census called Swan Upping to count the birds and check their health. Although she is not an active presence in politics, her influence is strong.

In her guise as a Queen, she has a wide variety of duties, from hosting diplomatic events to influencing trends. But one of her most important roles is as a philanthropist. Her life was set aside to serve others, so the position of Queen became a platform for her to fulfill her desires. When recognized the true faces of poverty around her, the impact on her part was such in a way that it would remain a tradition for centuries. She has worked as a patron for more than 600 charity organizations, and in which she served as an important figure for over 60 years. The organizations in which she served as patron includes British Red Cross, Cancer Research U.K., Save the Children U.K., and Blind Veterans U.K. , etc. From there, she tried to draw the attention of people in the country and the need to raise money for it. She is also partially involved in the events of these charities by making her appearance. Most members of the royal family are part of the charities, however, the Queen and her husband have been the patron of many organizations.

In 2012 alone, she was able to raise £1.4 million for those organizations. She also hosts various garden parties each year at Buckingham Palace to find ways to alleviate poverty. Also she served as an example as she donated money from her 90th birthday medal to 76 charities in her patronage. Through such actions, another form of her goodness is opened up to the society.

The year 2022 can be specially recorded in the life of Queen Elizabeth II and in the history of the British Royal Family. From February 6, 2022, the achievement of being the first British Monarch to celebrate the Platinum Jubilee would remain firmly at the top of the recognition series of everyone's favorite queen

Elizabeth II. She can be proud of being the first person to shine for 70 years as the head of the United Kingdom and the realms of the Commonwealth. It is another pleasure to be able to achieve this feat at the age of 95. The greatest noble position, not insignificant in history forever, has now become claimed by Her Majesty. They decided to celebrate it throughout the year.

The Queen spoke in an audio message, which broadcasted at the time, about the importance of keeping in touch with friends and families, as the enemy named Corona virus has been engulfed the world since 2019. The Queen was pleased with the role of technology in helping people connect with each other amid the global pandemic. She also paid tribute to the front-line workers who helped fight Covid-19 in the Commonwealth nations. She did not forget to convey the need for unity in the crucial situation.

Chapter 6 - Queen Elizabeth II's life in essence

Queen Elizabeth II is a distinguishable personality, who had been still the monarch of the United Kingdom and Commonwealth realms for seventy years. Even though she had to take over the position of Queen at the age of 27 unexpectedly, her attitude towards her role to handle it very responsibly and beautifully, is commendable. Whether as a ruler or as an individual, she shows through her actions that she is a success. It is generally said that it doesn't matter how many years a person has been in a position, but on what they have done over that time. If we look at the Queen here, we can say that she is great in both respects.

If a person has a good vision and has the determination to do it, then that person will be a good leader. Such a quality can be seen in Queen Elizabeth II. Addressing the nation on her 21st birthday, she shared a radio broadcast saying that her whole life, whether long or short, is for service and for the great imperial family we are all included. She does not limit it to mere words, she proves it with her actions. She shines the life of example on others through her every activity. When Queen entered the missions of that position, the nation was still suffering from the problems provided by World War II, and she slowly lifted everything back to normal. Hard work is one of her best qualities. There's no doubt that she is a great person who has been working hard for the nation with the same energy as before, even though she had crossed her 90s with age. Next, it's her commitment that makes her engaged on a hectic schedule. She also has the mindset to serve the whole world with her own nation.

Maybe because of such attributes and even better qualities, the face of Queen Elizabeth II can be seen as an example of being a leader with a smile full of contentment and love in everyone.

At a very young age, she was able to attract the attention of the people by doing good deeds while her father George V was King. Since then, she had interacted with the subjects from different sections, participated in hundreds of royal engagements, talked to people in England, visited across the Commonwealth on her vacations, and been involved on countless occasions, all these led for very few people to know the individual person within her. Although she is very close to her family, especially with her daughter Princess Anne and her grandchildren, Prince William, Prince Harry, and Princess Eugenie, she never revealed what she is thinking or her emotions in front of them. One of her virtues is that she does not combine personal and official life. But in some unavoidable situations, she had to make adjustments in one for another. Unexpectedly, the responsibility of the Queen came upon her soon after marriage following the demise of her father, and because of that she could not spend more time with her elder children. But she tried to enjoy the times she got to be with them as well as possible. During her childhood, she and her sister Margaret had to stay away from their parents for a while due to their official busy schedule. Growing up with grandparents, her parents realized that she had just developed a matured personality at her young age. She thus learned to adapt to circumstances. Her uncle Edward VIII had to get into the throne after the death of King George V but did not stay due to some personal issues. Thus, King George VI and then his daughter Queen Elizabeth II took over the duties.

When considering her as an individual away from formal affairs, you can see in her that she is a person who likes dogs, to drive horses, and then to drive cars fast. She has a quick sense of herself. In this advanced age, she is familiar with the technology. Princess Margaret is often said to have had a party girl image. But Elizabeth had not reached that level. The Queen is a glorious host who enjoys luxurious parties. She loves to receive and entertain guests and also knows how to ease them. She greets everyone from the top of the stairs at Buckingham Palace. She is able to manage both old and new friends together. Her ability to mix them up is also amazing. She would dance to her favorite tunes by Lester Lanin. His orchestra used to play at her parties as she likes that tune so much. She often accompanied her husband, Prince Philip, on a number of official trips. They were distant cousins and met for the first time in a family marriage in 1934 when Elizabeth was 8 and Prince Philip was 13. They met again at the Royal Naval College in 1939 and blossomed in love with each other at that young age. The relationship, which went unnoticed at home, and later Prince Philip approached King George VI for his blessings in 1946. Despite opposition from within the Palace, an official announcement was made in July 1947, and the wedding of Prince Philip and Queen Elizabeth II took place on 20 November 1947 at Westminster Abbey. It was an event that occurred in the Palace after World War II. In that relationship, they had four children. Her father, King George VI, died on February 6, 1952, and the couple was in Kenya at the time, so she could not be with him for the last time. She was crowned Queen or monarch of the United Kingdom and Commonwealth realms on June 2, 1953. It was held as a grand ceremony and at her suggestion it was telecast to be seen by people all over the world. She was also excellent in the role of a mother-in-law. When Prince Charles and Lady Diana got married after their love relationship, and later when they separated due to his connection with Camilla, and Diana was mentally down in it, it was the Queen who gave her full support and raised her. She was also deeply saddened by Diana's death. When Prince Philip retired from his official life, he sometimes assisted the Queen in her royal duties. At that time, the Queen delegated some of her responsibilities to Prince Charles and other senior members of the royal family. When Prince Philip, Duke of Edinburgh left them forever on April 9, 2021, she was mentally devastated. She lost her mother and sister in 2002, and as she learned to cope up with that pain, she managed to recover slowly from her love's farewell, albeit with great difficulty.

Queen Elizabeth II has the reputation of being the first royal female to join the army. She made her entry into defense during the horrors of the Second World War. She was only 19 years old at the time and trained as a military truck driver and mechanic. She continues her leadership with an emphasis on national identity, unity, and pride. She is an intelligent, smart, and quick-witted ruler. Queen Elizabeth II is the only person who can own the record of being the first ruler in British royal history even at the age of 95 to celebrate the Platinum Jubilee of her journey in the crown, surpassing Queen Victoria after her Silver Jubilee, Golden Jubilee.

Through Queen Elizabeth II, the nation has gained a monarch with stability, perseverance, and sense of duty.

Extras

A Humble Request

Our books are intended to indulge you. If you enjoyed this book or gained any valuable information from it in any way, feel free to share your experience with us. Your contented reviews will help to boost us not only in the sales perspective but also to improve our creativity. Please leave a review at the store front where you purchased this book, and it would be greatly appreciated.

Related Books

Bob Mortimer, Vic Reeves, Their Comedy and Friendship

A journey through the life of Bob and Reeves, who mixed fun & amity in woe, joy and gave comic gifts. Grab your copy now.

https://www.amazon.com/dp/B09L5DH4BS

Dave Grohl, Melodic Nirvana of a Foo Fighter: Abridged Life Story of an American Music Legend, Dave Grohl

Feel the vibes of Dave Grohl who makes hex on instruments with bands and friends. Click for an exclusive experience.

https://www.amazon.com/dp/B09L5DXPJJ

Big Yin - Billy Connolly: Tale of Billy Connolly and the Way He Nourished His Willpower from Morbidity

Attain this book to know the tale of the survival of comic Big Yin, who bravely fought in front of ail which was sentenced that there's no cure.

https://www.amazon.com/dp/B09MNTN1VR

Can't Just Chuckle – The Richard Osman Book: Unofficial Guide to the monumental moments of The English comedian Richard Osman's Life, In Short

This quietly moving book is the quick read on the towering Richard Osman, the Pointless guy whose debut book is breaking all records. Get a copy!

https://www.amazon.com/dp/B097NJ3QML

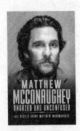

Matthew McConaughey, Undazed and Unconfused: All rights about Matthew McConaughey

To know all about the quintessential Texan Mathew McConaughey, his quest to find the meaning of life, how he engineered his destiny-Buy the book.

https://www.amazon.com/dp/B098F9D3DF

I am Seth, Seth Rogen: The Life & Ventures of Seth Aaron Rogen

A book to make you laugh and think, a book to celebrate levity, grab a copy soon to know more about the man who made you laugh like a maniac!

https://www.amazon.com/dp/B0977M74ZT

Sinéad O'Connor, The Unofficial Biography: Sinead O'Connor's Life Story In Short

Sinead O'Connor stole Prince's song, became a star; then destroyed her career. BUY a copy NOW to read the story of the most controversial pop star.

https://www.amazon.com/dp/B098MTR4LL

Andrew McCarthy, Dwelling Down Into 80's Brat Pack Era: A Nostalgic Memoir

Hunting high and low for a nostalgia-inducing book to immerse yourself in the 80s world? Get the book to know about Andrew McCarthy, the Brat Packer.

https://www.amazon.com/dp/B096F13S1W

Being Billie: Billie Eilish, A Short Life Story

Dark, but poignantly so, like Billie Eilish's songs, this book brings you her life's trials and triumphs in a candid narration. Buy a copy now!

https://www.amazon.com/dp/B095WXTGK3

Will Power Smith: Will Smith's Way to Success

Grab your copy to be inspired by the life of Will Smith, who came from rap-acting, faced strains & won success, beaten his sad infancy & other chains.

https://www.amazon.com/dp/B09RQ6ZPNP

THE END

THE END

Made in the USA
Monee, IL
01 February 2024